MW00569344

When Hope Wins

Marli Spieker

To Bonnie,
with gratitude &
Hope! Marli Spieker
Rom 15:13

When Hope Wins

Cover and Interior Design by Liquid Lotus LLC
Photographic images by Marli Spieker except for chapter 8 which was provided by Marlene de Fatima Vasques.
Some of the anecdotal illustrations in this book are true-to-life and are included with the permission of the persons involved. All other illustrations are composites of real situations, and any resemblance to people living or dead is coincidental.

Printed in China
1 2 3 4 5 6 7 8 / 14 13 12 11 10

To my husband Edmund

It has been a delightful adventure to live for 44 years with your German head and your Brazilian heart! Like no other, you have taught me to believe in Hope's ultimate win. Thank you for carrying me in your prayers, sharing your godly wisdom, and sacrificially loving me—and Project Hannah!

To each woman ministering in Project Hannah's worldwide teams, and to the precious women God has given us to serve.

You have taught me to embrace courage without counting the cost and to pray expectantly until Hope wins in the midst of hopelessness and despair! Thank you for your amazing resilience and example!

Soli Deo Gloria!

Contents

Foreword	7
Preface	9
Chapter 1 ... Lives are Changed! (Marli)	10
Chapter 2 ... There is Truth! (Alpana)	36
Chapter 3 ... There is Love! (Bukuria)	48
Chapter 4 ... There is Grace! (Katja)	62
Chapter 5 ... There is Healing! (Ella)	74
Chapter 6 ... There is Strength! (Justina)	90
Chapter 7 ... There is Freedom! (Ramona)	104
Chapter 8 ... There is Redemption! (Marlene)	118
Chapter 9 ... There is Wisdom! (Buakab)	136
Chapter 10 ... There is Infinite Mercy! (Marli)	156
Epilogue	170
About the Author	173
Project Hannah : A Ministry of TWR	174

Foreword

by Gracia Burnham

This is a book about real women—and their real life testimonies. And we all know that real life is, at times, messy and confusing.

I will always be grateful for that young woman in Boston in the book-signing line who asked me, "How can I pray for you?" I was used to people telling me how earnestly they had prayed for my husband Martin, and me while we were held hostage by extremists in the jungles of the Philippines. Our year-long captivity had caught the eye of the media and the Christian community, and many prayed because of the publicity of our story.

But here was an intercessor who wanted to know, "How can I pray for you?" I told her about the strange burden for hurting women in the world that had descended on me several weeks before. "I just don't know what to do with this burden," I told her. She said, "Have you heard about Project Hannah?" She told me to do an Internet search when I got home. And that was the beginning of my involvement with Project Hannah and my friendship with Marli Spieker.

I have loved reading this book. I have learned something from each and every testimony. But you want to know the most encouraging sentence of the book for me? It was when Marli said, "When God called me to start Project Hannah, He never gave me a strategic plan—a business plan." All she knew was that she had an unshakeable burden to help suffering women all over the world. And look at what God has done with that burden!

How I so often wish that I were a "visionary," or a "dreamer." But I'm not. I am just me. A woman with an interesting story. The stories in *When Hope Wins* have encouraged me that God has given us all what we need to live a godly, abundant life (2 Peter 1:3, 4). God uses willing vessels whether they are "visionaries" or not. He can use anyone and any story. It is bittersweet to see how He often uses times of pain as a basis for a ministry.

I am in awe of these women—the ones you are going to read about. But more than that, I am in awe of our gracious God who uses our experiences and hardships to bring about good in our lives.

Thank you, Marli, for sharing these stories with us. Thank you for encouraging me—again—as you always do, to keep serving and trusting our good God. Our hope is in Him!

Preface

I cannot take any credit for writing the stories recorded in the book you hold in your hands. God wrote them all in eternity! I have simply gathered them and tried to put into words the deep feelings and memories echoing in the canyons of these dear women's souls.

This book is the result of collaborative work by colleagues and friends who have collected and translated countless testimonials and listener letters in numerous languages. I have also interviewed many people in an effort to keep the stories as accurate as possible.

Most of these stories are from women that I have met personally. There is no way to adequately thank each one of them for their generosity in allowing me a glimpse into the recesses of their hearts; to share their trials, their joys, and their hopes. For some the process was painful—it made them remember times of darkness and battles fought against hopelessness, fear, and abuse. They did so in the hope that somehow, someone would be touched and inspired by their stories.

I thank my dear friends and those Project Hannah team members whose stories are also recorded in this book. They courageously reveal the scars of their past to help their sisters see that hope wins!

Chapter 1

. . . Lives are Changed!

"But now, O Lord, You are our Father, We are the clay, and You our potter; And all of us are the work of Your hand."

—Isaiah 64:8

My life has been greatly enriched by my dear friends and Project Hannah team members as we have worked together to bring Hope to suffering women around the world. Looking back on my own life, I can see God's plan and purposes being fulfilled behind every experience, every season of my journey. Indeed, His grace never ceases to amaze me!

I was born into a humble Salvation Army missionary family in Brazil. I like to think that I was raised by my very own George Muller and Mother Teresa. My parents literally lived for God and for others. They took care of orphan boys, from the ages of four to eighteen, in a Salvation Army orphanage. So I grew up in a home full of boys, with three biological brothers and sixty-four other "brothers," many who were emotionally-damaged and from broken homes. That was a dangerous place for a little girl to be!

My mom worked tirelessly cooking, cleaning, washing, and caring for the basic needs of the boys with very little help. One day, as she was busy caring for the little ones, the phone rang. It was the police, who gave her the heartbreaking news that her 14-year-old son, Celso, had been killed by a truck while on his way home from school.

As my mom grieved for my brother, her mother's heart feared losing my brothers and me as well. She did not have enough hours in her day to give me the attention and care I needed, so she prayed for God to protect her only little girl. He answered through a scholarship I received to attend an elite all-girls' Episcopal boarding school in the city. I went there when I was only five years old.

Although the school offered me a pristine education, life itself was not so pristine. My parents were poor missionaries . . . the other girls' parents were wealthy farmers, business owners, and politicians. I faced overt prejudice and, at times, even emotional abuse. I remember often being forced by one of the bullies to do her homework!

It was there that I learned to love art, beauty, music, and all the social graces, as well as God's Word. And even though I am thankful to God for giving me that valuable experience, the truth is that I never really quite fit in. Seven years later, I returned home to find out that I did not fit into my own family either. My two brothers were amazing young men, full of life and serving side by side with my parents in the orphanage. I was different. The long years away from home had taken their toll. By the time I came home, I was a very insecure teenager struggling with feelings of inadequacy and rejection.

One winter night, sad and tired, I made a bargain with God. I said, "Lord, if You will take away these awful feelings and fill me with Your love and joy instead, I will give you all of me . . . my whole life to serve you until the day I die." God took me up on my word. He took away the negative feelings and sadness; He gave me His pardon and peace. Joy and hope I had never known before flooded my soul and have stayed with me even through my darkest nights. By His grace I have kept my part of the deal, and He has fulfilled every single one of His promises to me!

So, at age seventeen, and below the normal acceptance age, I was accepted at the Salvation Army Cadet School. Immediately I became involved in their tremendous social ministry working in the slums, brothels, and bars of big Brazilian cities such as Sao Paulo, Belo Horizonte, and others. I was doing exactly what I had seen my parents do—embodying Christ's message to bind up the brokenhearted, to preach the good news to the poor, and give hope to the hopeless—feeding them, loving them, and leading them to Jesus. I loved every moment of it!

When I was nineteen, I became engaged to be married to a handsome, intelligent Danish missionary, who was ten years my senior. Eight days before our wedding day, with final preparations in full swing, the phone rang. I listened in shock as my fiancé told me that he was calling off the wedding because he did not love me anymore—a dramatic end to our four-year relationship. He left the ministry, and me, to run away with my friend and maid of "honor"!

My life and dreams were shattered. I could barely breathe. I learned the hard way that love can hurt. Wrestling again with feelings of rejection, abandonment, and betrayal, I knew only one place to go. As an act of my will, not my emotions, I heard myself saying, "Lord, I do not understand, but I have given my life to you. Your will, not mine be done." Fleeing to Jesus' arms, I waited until healing began, immersing myself in serving those whose problems were immeasurably greater than mine. Through those painful years, only the certainty that "underneath are the everlasting arms of Jesus" kept me going. I stayed there until healing came and I was able to walk on my own again.

I began to understand the great truth that God is my maker—never my destroyer. He sustained me in ways I still cannot explain. That was the beginning of a long process of trusting, obeying, and abandoning myself into His hands, no matter what. It was then that I experienced "up close and personal" that Jesus is the great healer of the human soul! He not only healed me, but as I served others I saw that same healing mercy and power putting other broken lives, broken dreams, broken families, and broken hearts back together. And with His healing came the certainty that He has a plan—a plan for "welfare and not for calamity," a plan to give me "a future and a hope," (Jeremiah 29:11).

And what a future and hope! Not too long after that painful experience, God rewarded me with Edmund, a German seminary student, who became my closest friend and loving husband; a man of integrity, a truly unusual young man! We share the same passion for God and compassion for the lost. Together, through thick and thin, we have served the Lord every day of our married lives—for more than four decades.

Two years later, after having our first little boy, Marcio, Edmund and I joined Trans World Radio (TWR). Our first assignment was to establish the radio ministry in Brazil. Fourteen years and two more children later, we were called to join TWR's International team. We left Brazil and everything familiar to us, and moved to Canada to raise our personal support and to learn English. I was 39 years old.

That was a turning point for our family. To this day, we still cherish our Canadian brothers and sisters who embraced us, loved our children, and walked with us into our new life and ministry.

After two years in Canada, we moved to Chatham, New Jersey. Edmund became the TWR International Director for Asia Pacific and started traveling extensively. For ten years he led the ministry there while I stayed home in the United States raising our children and being his "support staff."

Finally, after our two younger children were both married within four months of each other, Edmund asked me to join him in Asia. "But what will I do there?" I asked. TWR was not inviting me to be involved in the Asian ministry . . . only Edmund! He answered, "I don't know . . . but you will see. God has something beautiful for you to do there." That was one of the first times in our marriage that my German husband did not have a specific answer for my question. But that vague response turned out to be one of his most accurate ever!

So, after much praying and soul searching, I agreed to go. I flew to Hong Kong and from there we went to the island of Guam where TWR has its powerful transmitters and studios beaming the gospel to all of Asia, but particularly to China. It is important to me to always know where I am going, and how I am going to get there. With this huge change in our lives, I knew nothing—and neither did my wise husband! All he knew was that God had "something wonderful" for me to do. But I usually have a plan B and C in my pocket, just in case! So, I began to present these elaborate plans to the Lord.

The truth is that I did not want to leave behind the new mentoring ministry for young mothers we had started in our church . . . or our first grandson . . . or our beautiful, secure little home in the US. But I went, believing in God's unknown "plan and future" for me.

Sure enough, there was nothing for me to do! The next morning, after I dropped Edmund off at the TWR office, I took my Bible and drove to a beautiful deserted beach. I needed to spend time alone with God, to feel His nearness . . . the assurance that I was still in the center of His love. I asked Him to speak to me, so I opened the Bible and my eyes immediately fell on Jeremiah 18, *"Go down to the potter's house . . . Behold, like the clay in the potter's hand, so are you in My hand . . ."*(Jeremiah 18:2, 6). The words flashed like neon lights in my mind. I knew what was coming, so I immediately closed the Bible. This was not the message I wanted to hear!

Let me turn to Isaiah, my favorite prophet, I thought. Turning a few pages these words from

Isaiah 64:8 now seemed to light up: *"But now, O Lord, You are our Father, We are the clay, and You our potter; And all of us are the work of Your hand."* I quickly closed my Bible again. I was just a little girl when I had heard my dad preaching about this for the first time!

Stubbornly I continued . . . maybe the New Testament would have what I was looking for. Dear old Paul wrote a lot about God's love. Romans . . . *yes . . . this was better. "Who will separate us from the love of Christ?"* (Romans 8:35). Now this is what I wanted to hear! So I kept reading, drinking in each word's meaning with all my soul. I was so engrossed in that glorious passage that I kept reading on into Chapter 9. Suddenly, verse 20 jumped out at me as though it had been laying in wait around the corner. *"Who are you, O man, who answers back to God? The thing molded will not say to the molder, 'Why did you make me like this,' will it?"* But God was still not finished: *"**Or does not the potter have a right over the clay**?"* (Romans 9:20-21).

In that moment my little car became a sanctuary. I felt as though God was sitting in the passenger's seat staring at me! I came to my senses. In tears, I relinquished all my rights, my plans, and my will to Him. "Yes, I am the clay, Lord." And in my mind and heart I knew that clay does not rebel; clay does not have plan A, B, and C; clay does not talk back to its maker! It simply abandons itself to the shaping of the potter's hands.

I thought I was a flexible person. I was willing to go back and forth to Asia as many times as needed. We had sold our house so that we could use the mortgage payments to provide for my personal expenses traveling with Edmund. I had left behind family, church, personal comforts . . . but God did not want my "flexibility." He wanted my "pliability;" my total abandonment to His will and His skillful hands to shape me according to His plan—not mine! So, after thirty-two years of missionary service, I found myself surrendering my life anew to His sovereign will.

A few days later we were in Singapore; Edmund as busy as ever and with the "Martha" in me still with nothing to do! I decided to take the city bus and crisscrossed Singapore watching the beautiful Chinese, Indian, Malaysian, and even a few Caucasian women passing by on the sidewalks.

One day I was making a call from a phone booth in a shopping center, when the automatic door next to me swung open and a couple walked in, followed by a blast of hot air. Singapore sits right on top of the equator—the heat and humidity are suffocating! The woman was dressed in black from head to toe, with only a little net peephole for her eyes. Her husband though, was wearing a cool, comfortable cotton T-shirt! I have never been able to forget that disturbing sight.

Very grieved in my spirit I cried out, "God! How can this be?" I imagined how the woman must feel under her black burka in that unbearable heat. I sat down in the mall for a long time. That's when I sensed God asking me, "Did you see that black veil? It is not only over her head, it is over her mind, her heart, her family, her spirit—her whole life! This woman lives in darkness!"

My answer was, "Lord, whatever You want me to do to bring her into Your light I will do it! Just tell me how! Then I felt Him say, "What is the closest thing available to you? What do you have in your hand?" *A microphone. Radio. Trans World Radio!* I knew the power of radio! Its waves can go where missionaries can't! It penetrates any man-made barrier, whether geographical, political, ideological, or religious. And even today, radio continues to be a very effective mass media communication tool!

From that day on God started pouring information about the plight of women around the world into my lap. I learned that for countless women today, the world is indeed a dark and dangerous place. Women are still disproportionately impacted by the horrors of wars that never seem to end, natural disasters that steal their families and homes, illiteracy, diseases that ravage their bodies, and poverty that leaves them struggling merely to survive. And the spiritual darkness in which these women live is even greater than their physical plight.

"But why, God?" I asked. "Why throughout the ages, in every culture, do women face such suffering?" God reminded me of Genesis 3:15 when Satan deceived Eve. I found it interesting—the serpent never even addressed Adam, the one in charge of everything, the head of the family. The one who named all the animals, including the serpent! Satan knew that Eve would turn around and convince her husband to eat the forbidden fruit and disobey God. It occurred to me that Adam's participation in this most important event in human history is described in Genesis 3 with only three little words: "*. . . And he ate.*" Just that. Nothing else. No questions asked. No reasoning, nothing!

Satan knew then, that God gave authority to men, but to women He gave the powerful gift of ***influence***. Every baby girl comes wrapped in it! All of humanity must first pass through the body and soul of a woman. It spends its most formative years under her influence.

It is amazing, that even after Eve's fiasco, God is still counting on the woman to be His partner in His miracle of creation. Every day! She is the entry to life. She leaves fingerprints all over her children's lives. Pascal said so well, "The hand that rocks the cradle, directs the destiny of the world." So very true!

No wonder Satan—the first abuser—targeted Eve for his destructive purposes. To this day he continues to break the bodies, souls, and spirits of women all over the world. In more than seventy countries I have seen broken women producing broken children; and broken children turn into broken adults who produce broken societies!

In many cultures it is said that women suffer "from the womb to the tomb." In some countries, if a baby girl can take her first breath she has already beaten the odds. Countless baby girls are systematically aborted for social, political, or economic reasons. Worldwide, the great majority of women are the least valued, the least fed, the least educated, and certainly the least reached with the gospel of our Lord Jesus.

Reading further in Genesis 3:15, I found the answer to my question. God said, "*And I will put enmity between you and the woman, and between your seed and her seed.*" This curse, this "enmity" between Satan and the woman is the reason that women have historically been the victims of violence, incest, abuse, abortion, and all sorts of other crimes. However, in the same breath, God promised the "seed of the woman"—Jesus Christ, the great liberator of the oppressed who became a curse for us on the cross. As it says in Galatians 3:13,"*Cursed is everyone who hangs on a tree.*"

It occurred to me that women's suffering is not only a gender problem, or just a social or economic problem, it is a deeply rooted ***spiritual*** problem that can only be dealt with through spiritual means. I knew that the only way to go about releasing women from darkness was through prayer—the most powerful resource God has given to His Church. Corporate, focused, informed, earnest prayer!

The strategy for Project Hannah was given to me in that mall, when I not only saw the use of the radio in a new light, but understood anew that *prayer* is the most important work we can do for these dear women. I am an eyewitness to His power-working miracles in the lives of women from many cultures and walks of life, as a direct result of our prayer and culturally-relevant radio programs. All the stories of this book testify to that. Project

Hannah's massive worldwide prayer movement is the propelling force behind such miracles. In Project Hannah we believe that prayer not only supports the work—prayer *is* the work!

I never imagined that God would take my small, faithful prayer group in Singapore, made up of twelve Chinese praying friends, and raise intercessors in over 105 countries! There is now literally a wave of prayer around the globe 24/7. Together, we storm the gates of hell on behalf of these women, using a simple and powerful prayer calendar that has been translated into more than forty languages!

Each month we focus on one country or people group, or a women's issue such as the effects of war, domestic violence, poverty, women in prison, illiteracy, physical and spiritual bondage, etc. Project Hannah's intercessors—Christian men, women, and young people around the world—pray in unison the same prayer request for every day of the month. They are moving God's arm, to change women's hearts, heal their bodies and their families, and restore their dignity.

Project Hannah's signature program, *Women of Hope,* is broadcast today in more than 50 languages on radio, on the Internet, and other media. Through it we enlighten women, impacting their world with God's worldview. We tell them how precious and valued they are in God's sight. How He gave His only ***son***—not a daughter—to save each one of them. That Jesus Christ, "the seed of the woman," has come "to destroy the works of the devil," (1 John 3:8). He came to deliver women from the power of the enemy of their souls! That Jesus became "a curse" for us "on the tree." And that Jesus Himself said, *"So if the Son makes you free, you will be* *free indeed,"* (John 8:36). That is the liberating, victorious message we have to tell women everywhere!

Since Project Hannah's beginning, we have strived to scale cultural, religious, social and racial barriers using these two powerful tools—superpower radio and high-power prayer. God is using our efforts and taking women out of darkness into the light of Jesus . . . and ***hope*** wins all over the world!

- Project Hannah was born in my heart in that little old car in Guam when I surrendered anew my will and plans to God.
- Project Hannah was sealed in my heart at that shopping mall when so patiently, so clearly, so tenderly God gave me His strategy.

- Prayer is the backbone!
- Radio programs are the voice!
- Awareness and mercy ministries are Project Hannah in the flesh living out Jesus' message.

It is very humbling to see God's redemptive work succeed on such a tremendous scale! It takes me back to my youth in Curitiba, South Brazil, when I surrendered my life and my will completely to serve Jesus for as long as I lived. If I lived a thousand lives, I would give them all to my King Jesus. For there is nothing greater, nothing more fulfilling or rewarding than to be clay in the potter's hand. What a beautiful thing!

Chapter 2

. . . There is Truth!

"So will My word be which goes forth from My mouth; It will not return to Me empty, Without accomplishing what I desire, And without succeeding in the matter for which I sent it."

—Isaiah 55:11

To be born into a Hindu family is to be a Hindu. There is no other choice—you live like a Hindu, and you die like one. And like countless others, Alpana's family took Hinduism very seriously. Every day they worshipped millions of gods and goddesses, along with things in nature. They performed daily rituals, attended all of the religious festivals, and sacrificed animals to please the gods and goddesses.

From a young age, Alpana was taught to believe in reincarnation—the transmigration of the soul. She was told that how she lived now would determine her status in the next life, as well as how many times she would have to come back to this world.

As a little girl, I remember listening to people talk in our village about the "one true God." I was intrigued. *Why is my family worshiping so many gods and goddesses, if there is only one true God?* I wondered. It did not make sense to me.

When I was sixteen, my father purchased a radio. We loved to listen to news, music, and Hindi songs together. One day I found a Christian Hindi program. The speaker was Pastor John Lal and he was talking about the *one true God* that I had wanted to know about for so long! At last, I was getting some answers to my many questions about Him. From then on I listened to that program every single day. I could not get enough of it!

One day when I was alone at home, Pastor Lal was teaching from Romans 1:19–25, which talks about idols. He explained clearly why idol worship is wrong. I was curious and listened attentively to the entire program. Then he explained how the true God wants to have a relationship with each person; how He sent His Son Jesus to live here like one of us, and to die on the cross to pay for all our sins. He came to give us peace and forgiveness and then, after we die, to take us to Heaven to live forever with Him.

That made sense! *If this is true*, I thought, *then why all the rituals, and sacrifices, and offerings? I will never come back to this planet again!* It was so clear to me. My salvation does not depend on my efforts, but on God's power to forgive me—an idol worshiper and a sinner. I wanted to worship this God and His Son Jesus. When the pastor asked if I wanted to pray with him to accept Jesus, I did. I said, "Oh God, I have sinned against you. Please forgive my sins!"

This true God gave me something I had never received from any of the millions of gods I had so faithfully worshipped for years. Peace and joy—to me? An idol worshiper? I felt accepted, loved, and complete! In exchange, I gave myself totally to Jesus. Never had I sensed this kind of closeness to the gods I had worshiped all my life. Never had I wept before them. And yet now tears of joy began streaming down my face.

I continued listening to the broadcasts, thinking, *If my family knew what I was doing, I would be in big trouble!* Time went by and every day I learned something new. I learned to pray for my family that they too, would find this one true God. I desperately wanted a Bible so I could read about God for myself, but had no idea where I could get one. So, I prayed for a miracle. When the radio station offered a Bible, I was excited and gladly accepted one. I could now do their Bible Correspondence Course.

I secretly continued to study Scripture and learned that eating food my family offered to the idols was wrong, so I did not eat it anymore. I felt a strong aversion to the rituals that had been second nature to me for so long! I also decided not to participate in the festivals. In fact, I told my siblings that what they were doing was not right.

After five months, I mustered the courage to tell my family about my newfound faith. They did not like it at all. One by one they turned against me. Especially my father—he was furious! He locked the radio away in a box. I was not allowed to touch it or to speak about this new religion. My parents took me out of school and tried to isolate me from everyone and everything important to me. They threatened to marry me off to an older Hindu man. The persecution within my own family made my life a living nightmare! My only solace and comfort was in praying to God. He was always there. He never left me, even for a moment. The more they persecuted me, the greater my determination became to never go back to Hinduism.

So I began praying for a second miracle—another radio. Amazingly, after only fifteen days, the mail-man brought a new radio to our house! To this day I have no idea who sent that radio to me, but my father was so angry that he told the mailman to take the radio back to where it came from. I just prayed and prayed asking God to give my father a change of heart.

Where I live, if a package is not received, the postmaster keeps it for a week before returning it to the sender. Just one day before the week was over, my father went and retrieved the radio from the post office and gave it to me! Without any explanation, he said I could listen to the radio again. I was so thankful, I wept. This was God's doing and I knew it!

I explained to my parents why I wanted to listen to the radio so badly. And this time they listened patiently to me, even though they continued with their Hindu beliefs. As I began to share with my mother about my faith, she let me read the stories of Jesus' miracles in John's gospel. She was intrigued by them and wanted to hear more.

It just "happened" that a few days later she became very ill. I knew God could heal her miraculously, so I said, "Mother, I know God can heal you if you will just pray to Him." Of course she did not know how to pray, but she asked me to pray for her. I prayed for God to heal her . . . and He did! My mother began to feel better. She believed that Jesus' power had healed her. My whole family saw God's power in her healing. Not too long after this, God performed an even greater miracle in her life. She accepted Jesus and believed in this one true God who had healed her. Now I was not alone!

My mother destroyed all the idols in the house. (It is usually the mothers who are more ritualistic in

Hindu families.) She also began sharing her faith with my father. He had noticed that when we prayed God would answer us. He saw the transformation in our lives and he could not deny God's power in us. The day finally came for yet another miracle when he too surrendered his life to God.

For years the radio had been my sole source of fellowship and biblical instruction. It was three years after my father's conversion when all of us as a family began attending a Christian church. What a joy that was for me! Gone now are the days of offering food to idols, performing meaningless rituals, and sacrificing animals to please gods and goddesses who have no power. Now my whole family is free from "the dominion of darkness" and is living in God's light. We all worship the only God worthy of our praise.

Project Hannah has given me the joy of meeting our listeners face to face. When I get requests from women in distress, God burdens my heart to pray for them right away. I pray they will leave their idols behind and follow the *one true God.* Only then will they know the *Truth*—how precious they are in His sight. No other god values women as our God, and Jesus Christ His Son.

Through suffering and persecution, God prepared Alpana to be His witness, to comfort and guide many women still walking in darkness all over India. He used two things to keep her growing in her faith and knowledge of God's word—radio and the Christian counseling she received from TWR India's follow-up workers.

It is no surprise that today through Project Hannah's ministry, Alpana uses these two very powerful tools as she ministers to Hindi-speaking women, the majority of whom are abused and oppressed in their own homes. She counsels them through letters and phone calls just like someone did for her years ago. She knows the emptiness they feel. She also helps to set up listener rallies, and lends her soft voice to the recordings of our *Women of Hope* program segments. Having experienced the power of prayer, Alpana now sends out Project Hannah's Hindi prayer calendars to women, knowing full well the great potential they have as intercessors.

Chapter 3

. . . There is Love!

"HE UPHOLDS THE CAUSE OF THE OPPRESSED AND GIVES FOOD TO THE HUNGRY. . . . THE LORD WATCHES OVER THE ALIEN AND SUSTAINS THE FATHERLESS AND THE WIDOW."

—PSALM 146:7,9 NIV

March 15, 2008 will be remembered in Albanian history as the day when death rained down from the sky in the form of bullets, missiles, shells, and rocks. Video footage broadcast on Albanian television showed a massive fireball shooting up toward the sky as shrapnel and shell fragments rained down on homes and vehicles. Many Albanians lost their lives, and thousands more lost their homes and businesses.

But this was not collateral damage in a military conflict—for Albania was not at war! The government had inherited more than 100,000 tons of excess ammunition from the former communist regime and the outdated weapons were stored in former army depots across the country, marked for destruction. An unexpected blast at the depot in Gerdec, a village about six miles north of the capital, Tirana, set off a series of explosions, and ammunition continued to detonate long into the night.

Enkelejda Kumaraku, director of TWR's Albanian partner ministry who coordinates Project Hannah there, and her team were among the very few media representatives who were granted access to the village immediately after the explosion. Their report began airing right away, sending messages of comfort to the victims and reporting their stories and needs. Soon, they were inundated with messages from all over Tirana asking for prayer. Enkelejda and her staff were first responders and continued their labor of love—offering the comfort and hope that only God can give in such desperate circumstances.

Six months after this terrible tragedy occurred, Enkelejda extended an invitation to visit her country. With my husband and also my dear friend Janet Broling along for the journey, Enkelejda took us to visit a small village that was situated on the opposite side of the mountain where the explosion had occurred.

We set out early in the morning, but the temperature was already quite high. Riding through the chaotic traffic, we would stop and pray for the women we met. Along the way, Enkelejda told us about the work that was being done in the village and also about the story of one very special woman.

We have visited the village quite often since the explosion. Every week volunteers from a church in Durres, where Project Hannah has approximately eighty intercessors, bring food, clothes, and other items to help them rebuild their homes and lives. They have experienced God's love in flesh and blood!

I met Bukuria shortly after the explosion. Her name means "beautiful," but the first time I interviewed her, I remember thinking, *Now I know what hopelessness looks like.* She was so traumatized we had to stop several times, as she was overcome by tears. However, through the tears, grief, and desperation, I could see that this woman has courage of steel. Like a true "mama bear" she is fiercely protecting her only treasure—her 10 children. Her whole focus, against all odds, is to somehow help them succeed, to give them a better life.

She works so very hard in the fields from sunrise to sunset! Then she goes and sells her produce in the city streets. As we talked together I realized that even though she cannot read or write, she is not only courageous, but a wise woman with high moral values that she is passing on to her children.

Bukuria is in her forties but she looks sixty! All that she has been through, including raising 10 children on her own has taken its toll. She told me how she and her husband had decided to leave their village in Northern Albania and move to this area. Like many of their friends fleeing from the harsh winters that isolate them from the rest of the country for months, they had hoped to give their children a better life. So they sold everything and bought a small property in this village.

Only six months after they had settled in their new home, her husband was diagnosed with terminal cancer. He lost the battle after a time and passed away, leaving her alone to take care of their children and her elderly father who was living with her. Bukuria said, "I used to comfort myself that even though things were bad—sometimes we did not have enough food for all of us—at least we had a roof over our heads, and beds to sleep in at night. But then the explosion happened, and my house and my hopes were blown away. Two weeks later, when it seemed that things could not get worse, my father passed away because of injuries he received during the explosion."

Hopelessness was written all over her face. But when that interview went on the air, it changed everything!

God was watching over Bukuria. It just "happened" that one of the directors of Hope for Albania—a Dutch Christian organization serving Albanians in a variety of ways, including construction—was stuck in traffic listening to the radio and heard Bukuria's story. He was so touched by it that he immediately called our office and said that Hope for Albania would rebuild this widow's house. Construction began the very next day and did not stop until the house was finished!

I know from personal experience that God is *Jehovah Jirah*—our Provider—that He never sleeps and never slumbers, and that He is the father of the fatherless and the husband of widows. Yet, when I saw God stepping into this woman's terrible circumstances using a radio program in the middle of a traffic jam to help her, I felt privileged that He chose to use us as a catalyst for this miracle.

Every house in that village was damaged, some more than others, but none as badly as Bukuria's. Even the villagers agreed that she should be the one to get the most help. Building her new house took a few months, but closing the hole in her heart and calming her fears and uncertainties will take much longer.

But Bukuria's meeting with Hope has put a smile back on her leathery face. She knows now that it was

God who led us to help her. She also knows that we love Him, and that He is loving her and her children through us! With the new house she also received a new radio; now she listens regularly to the *Women of Hope* programs. She hears God's life-changing message on the radio and sees her new friends embodying Jesus' love. Today, some members of the Project Hannah prayer group in Durres even run a Vacation Bible School with all the village children—the first ever in this village!

It is just a matter of time . . . one of these days Jesus will walk into her heart and give her a total makeover—not just of her house, but her whole life!

We arrived at the village to find women and children waiting for us along the side of the unpaved road. They were ecstatic to see Enkelejda and as we visited various homes, the warm Albanian hospitality was lavishly poured out on all of us, with many hugs, kisses, and smiles.

First, we went to visit Bukuria's white house. It was really beautiful! Knowing its story I had to fight back tears as we were given a tour by her daughters—four beautiful, intelligent young women ranging in age from 15 to 24 years. My heart ached for these young girls, trapped in that village with no way to further their education or to find a job, or even a good marriage prospect. So much wasted potential!

That afternoon a meeting was planned at another home that had been damaged. Enkelejda asked me to share with the women that they are precious in God's sight and He values them so much He sent His Son Jesus to die for them. She hoped that after being shown God's love and provision for the past six months they might respond to the gospel message.

The house was packed with women, young and old, waiting for us. I will never forget the eyes of an old widow sitting at my side. Not once did she smile! Her empty eyes reflected her empty soul. She was surrounded by broken walls and broken dreams, with no faith to sustain her. I thought, *This dear widow needs more than food and shelter. She needs hope—she needs Jesus!*

At the end of the meeting I asked if they wanted to have their sins forgiven, to be given a new hope and hearts full of God's love. To my surprise, they all said yes! But when I asked them to pray with me, a deathly silence filled the room. After a while, two of the younger women said, "We cannot pray to Jesus today because we are in the midst of Ramadan."

These desperately needy women, bound by religious tradition, believe that they are powerless to decide their own soul's destiny. To me they were the embodiment of helplessness! That old widow, even in the midst of her darkness, rejected hope—God Himself, and so did all of the others!

When we finished the meeting, all of the women wanted us to visit their homes as well. But our time with them had come to an end. As we went to the car, women and children walked close beside us in a procession, holding our arms, laughing and trying to communicate with us all at the same time. Even though we could not speak their language they showed their appreciation for our visit—loving us through their smiles, hugs, and kisses. Within my soul I cried out to God, "When Lord? When will these women finally see your light, embrace your hope, and be set free?"

There were cracks forming in my heart—larger than the ones I had seen on their ceilings and walls. "Please, God," I cried out in my heart, "Please cause a greater explosion to shake this village again—an explosion of your powerful love and redemption in each of these women's hearts!"

I was comforted to remember that, unlike these women, we had met hundreds of others who had not rejected Jesus. They had embraced Him, experiencing the transforming power of our Lord Jesus. Their stories inspired me to continue fighting in this crusade of hope and love.

Chapter 4

. . . There is Grace!

"My grace is sufficient for you, for my power is made perfect in weakness."

—2 Corinthians 12:9 NIV

My Norwegian friend, Astrid, and I were at a small hotel room in Central Asia, thousands of miles away from home, sitting spellbound as we listened to Katja's courageous story, with the help of her interpreter, Katjana. Katja is indeed living proof of Hope's powerful victory over unbelief and the horrors of religious persecution. In the midst of tremendous suffering, God's grace surrounded her and her daughters—protecting, providing, surrounding them in sorrow and pain, as well as in times of joy.

I never imagined how much my decision to become a Christian would cost us. But, I do not regret it for a moment. You see, I could not understand what was wrong with me. After all, I had two beautiful girls, I prayed five times a day, gave money to the poor, and faithfully observed Ramadan. I did everything required of me—yet there was something missing in my life. I always felt empty inside. I could find no pleasure in anything. All my life I had searched for something, not knowing what it was. *What was wrong with me?* Then, my friend invited me to see a film about a man who could take away my sadness and give me joy instead. That was what I had been searching for—joy! So I agreed to go with her.

I tried to hide among the people so no one would recognize me. I was so nervous that I was afraid others would hear the pounding of my heart. But as I watched the movie, I began to relax . . . just a little. The man seemed to be speaking directly to me, as if I were the only person there. Something deep within me stirred.

By the end of the film I knew that this man was actually *Isa*—the Son of God! I understood that He was an innocent man, who willingly died to save the world. Far more importantly, I realized that He died for me—a simple woman! So I gave my life to Him. I did what they told us to do in the movie. At that moment I realized that everything my friend had said was true! All my life I had longed for this kind of joy; now Jesus filled me with it!

I could hardly wait to tell the women in my family what had happened to me. But within moments, the consequences of my decision hit home as they turned against me. "You are insane! What were you thinking?" they shouted. As their anger turned to hatred, their abuse quickly escalated from verbal to physical attacks and they beat me, and my girls too.

When I could stand it no longer, I complained to my husband. Instead of protecting me, he demanded, "What are you doing that they would treat you like that?" Though I was afraid, something within me would not allow me to lie, so I told him about the man in the film. I told him that I had become a Christian. His eyes locked upon mine. I saw them flash with fury and his contorted face clearly revealed his contempt for me. That's when he spewed out the most painful words I had ever heard, *"I divorce you, I divorce you, I divorce you! Take your daughters and get out of my house!"* he screamed. "Go! Go!!" In that instant my daughters and I were homeless and defenseless. That is how easily a Muslim man can divorce his wife in my culture.

As he pushed us out of the house, with nothing but the clothes we wore, the girls and I found ourselves alone on the streets. *Surely my parents will take us in,* I naively thought. But no . . . they too, wanted details.

Again, I could not lie, so I told them what had happened. My own parents looked at me and angrily shouted, "Who are you? Go away and don't come back! We do not know who you are anymore!"

Our only option now was to go to a government women's shelter. They asked me why I was on the streets. When they learned I had become a Christian, they simply said to me, "Christian? No . . . there is no room for you here!"

From that day on, my two children and I were homeless, penniless, and despised. I had no job and no family. At night we slept on the streets, or wherever we could find a place to hide. I had been a respected teacher but now I was totally destitute. We wandered from one village to the next living off the mercy of the few people who occasionally took pity on us.

Somehow in the midst of it all I found strength to go on. I kept saying, "God, why do I have to watch my daughters suffering this way? No one wants me; no one cares if we are alive or dead. Why?" But all through that terrible time I could feel that in spite of everything, we were never really alone. *Isa* was right there with us.

One day I desperately cried out, "God, please take me, and my daughters, out of these dangerous streets. Please protect us!" And He answered.

For days I had crossed paths with a beautiful, gentle woman at the market. She was different. She smiled a lot. Even when she was serious, she smiled with her eyes! She was full of joy, always optimistic. For some reason, she took a special interest in us. I thought, *I wish I had a sister like her!* When I asked her name, she said, "I am Katjana." I answered with excitement, "I am Katja!" She even had two girls the same age as mine!

As we talked together and I shared what had happened to us, she said, "I have a spare room where you can stay. Come with me. Our girls will get along just fine."

I could hardly believe what she was saying! But we went with her. Even Katjana's husband and daughters welcomed us. They freely shared whatever they had—food, beds, clothing—everything! She knew that I had been thrown out of my home because I had become a Christian, yet she did not seem to mind at all! I had never met people like this before.

I will never forget the day I learned the reason for her hospitality. We were alone when she pulled me close and whispered in my ear, "We love *Isa*, too. We are family now. Here . . . and forever." Now I was weeping for joy!

Sitting in that hotel room with those two remarkable women I wept as well. I kept thinking about what I would have done in Katja's place.

Would I have been so faithful in the face of such persecution? The day before, I had seen pictures of homes belonging to Christians that had been burned to the ground. I had met a Christian whose son had just been killed, and his livelihood—his horses—stolen. When he sought police protection, it was denied. They had become traitors in the eyes of their fellow man—totally rejected by their culture for the sake of Christ. But I was humbled and blessed. I saw how nothing could shatter their faith. Their fortitude came from the joy of the Lord. They trusted God in a way I have rarely seen in our comfortable culture. I had gone there to encourage them, but found I was the one encouraged—and challenged.

Katja and Katjana have gone through the fire of affliction and have eaten the bread of tears because of their faith. But God never wastes our tears. Those painful experiences are being used now to comfort others through the *Women of Hope* radio programs. They are telling women what *Isa* did for them and the joy and peace they now have! Their passion to rescue those still trapped in spiritual and cultural bondage is like a fire caught up in their bones. They want to bring hope to women kept by strict religious laws as "perpetual minors," forbidden to make any decisions for themselves.

When we finally said good night, Katja looked into my eyes and said, "Sister Marli, this thing you started (Project Hannah) is a good thing. It changed me. It changes my people. It blesses the women I minister to . . . not only over the radio, but in the villages and in the churches where I serve them. I wish all the women in my country could hear these programs and know that they are not alone. They need to know that there is someone who understands them. Our women need to find comfort and salvation in Isa alone. Jesus can make them free!"

My prayer that night was, "Thank you Lord for Your amazing grace—it is indeed sufficient for us. Your power is made perfect in weakness. Thank You for allowing me learn from these two remarkable women who are raising a new generation of *Women . . . of Hope!*"

Chapter 5

. . . There is Healing!

"A BRUISED REED HE WILL NOT BREAK, AND A SMOLDERING WICK HE WILL NOT SNUFF OUT."

—ISAIAH 42:3 NIV

How many times have I seen it? Regardless of circumstance, social status, or location, the story is always soaked in anger and tears. Occasionally, however, the storyteller's tears and anger have been wiped away by the hands of a miracle-working God and those who love Him. That's what happened to Ella, a brilliant Project Hannah program producer who is also a nurse, writer, mother, and Christian leader. To look at her today, you would never know that behind her beauty, talent, and efficiency lies a history of years of silent pain, shame, and deep emotional scars. But God carefully took care of

this "bruised reed" in an unusual way.

With my background in nursing and teaching, I never dreamed that one day God would use me in radio. I had never heard of Project Hannah, so I was surprised, although thankful, for the opportunity to use such a powerful medium to bring broken women to Jesus—the great Healer of broken hearts. But I never imagined that in serving with Project Hannah, He would have a surprise waiting for me.

In one of my first meetings with the Project Hannah team we were asked to tell our life story. Immediately, anxiety kicked in, *What do I say? How much do I tell? How can they possibly understand?* I had been told that there were some things in my past that I should never share with anyone. If I did, people would lose respect for me. But while believing it, part of me wondered. *How then do women deal with their hurts? Is keeping quiet working for them? It's not working for me!*

As I looked around the room and saw a group of spiritually-mature women, I made a decision to share everything. I thought to myself, *They hear all kinds of stories from women around them so surely they can handle my story! Maybe what I have been through can be the starting point for a discussion on how to reach women who are behind a barrier of shame and silence.* So I started, haltingly, with who I am, and where it all began.

I was five years old when my parents joined a mission organization and we moved to a new city. My school was located in a rough neighborhood and every morning, once the students arrived, the metal gates would slam shut behind us and we were actually locked in. Everyone thought we needed to be protected from the danger that surrounded the school. What no one knew about was the horror going on inside those gates.

Schoolwork would begin as normal. But then, on occasion, the principal would come to our classroom and choose two of us, taking us to another room where two men waited. There, under cover of darkness, the men molested us.

After each abuse, they would shove me into a walk-in closet until I stopped crying. Then I would huddle under the shelves filled with paper and chalk—crying, scared of the dark, frightened that the door would never open, yet terrified of what would happen when it did. The lies they told me played over and over in my mind—laughter, taunts, and lies that became the basis of how I saw myself and how I lived my life. "*Never tell, never say anything. No one will want to love you again if you tell. You are dirty. Your parents can't help you. They do not care. God can't help you, either. What does He care? He is not here stopping us, is He? This is all He made you for! No one will ever love you. You don't deserve love.*"

Childhood sexual abuse has always been shrouded in shame, pain, and silence. No one talked about it then. I think no one really knew to look out for it. My parents said that they noticed something was wrong, but they thought that I was reacting to the stress of moving to a new place and a new school.

One day when my father came to pick me up, I ran in fear from him. He found me hiding under a bench, shaking uncontrollably. That was it. He took me out of there. But the damage was done. My innocence and self-worth, even my understanding of God, stayed locked in that dark school closet. My mother grieved for the happy, talkative little girl she seemed to have lost. For years she wondered what had happened. But I would not talk. I did not tell. I did not think anyone would understand.

My parents headed out for their first missionary assignment in a different country. I enjoyed the place, made new friends, and learned a new language. My parents met with other missionaries on a regular basis for Bible studies and nights of prayer. The children were excused to play outside and since the yard was walled we did not need adult supervision—or so they thought. Out in the twilight though, I could see the adults crowded into the living room of the house praying or studying the Bible. I knew God was there with them in the light—why was He not also with me, out in the dark where that older boy was teaching us to play his version of "spin the bottle?" Those the bottle pointed to he would take off behind the banana trees to fondle and abuse. Week after week this happened—yet we said nothing to our parents. If we did speak up, we reckoned, no one would love us anymore because we were "dirty." I struggled with the question, *Why is this happening to me again?*

One of the hardest things for those who have been sexually abused is to make eye contact with people. As horrible as it all is, there is something in an abused child's heart that looks up to the abuser and wonders, "Do I have any value to you?" Almost wanting to be loved by the abuser. But the disgust in the eyes that look back—the abuser having taken what they want—always told me that I was only a piece of dirty garbage to them. An abused child hangs her head, never wanting to meet someone's eyes.

Even though I was taught that God cherished and valued me, I still was afraid to look up at Him—certain that I would see rejection in His eyes. The painful experiences in my past distorted my view of the world, of people, and even of God. I wanted Him, but I mistakenly thought, *Why would He ever want me?* I had given my heart to Jesus and I knew my sins were forgiven, but I didn't know I was perfect in His sight! I prayed. I read my

Bible. Later I even felt called to attend Bible school. Yet, I never dealt with the sins committed against me, with the pain and distorted perceptions locked up inside me.

Years went by. One day as I read my Bible I stopped at Ezekiel 36:25-27 which says, "Then I will sprinkle clean water on you, and you will be clean; I will cleanse you from all your filthiness and from all your idols. Moreover, I will give you a new heart and put a new spirit within you; and I will remove the heart of stone from your flesh and give you a heart of flesh. I will put My Spirit within you and cause you to walk in My statutes, and you will be careful to observe My ordinances."

I started to cry, "God you know how I want to be washed, to have a new heart, to be able to feel again. I want to be caused to walk with You." I was so tired of struggling on my own. God answered me by bringing a number of caring people into my life. Some came for a short time, while others stayed by my side for years—

walking with me, carrying my pain. Wounded people need to see God's love in real flesh and blood. Like Thomas . . . I needed to see and touch.

One day I had the courage to look up at God and ask, "Lord, where were You?" He said, "Little one, I was there holding you, covering your eyes with my hands. My tears dripped on your face, and I felt your hurt with you." In that moment, I knew that I had never been abandoned. So I began to look up and meet the eyes of the One who loves me even with the scars in my soul.

I always thought I would be too scarred to be of any use. I was wrong. God is using my scars to help other women in far away places. In the very beginning of this journey I often prayed a simple prayer: "God, take me through the pain, walk me through the hard ways, but please, when You bring me out of this pain, let me bring others out with me." In His love and faithfulness, that is what He is doing today.

As I finished my story and looked around the room, I wasn't prepared for what I saw. My Project Hannah friends were in tears. That puzzled me. I had heard some of their stories—the bad decisions they had made, the terrible abuse some had endured before, and in some cases after, they became believers; but despite it all, they were happy. It seemed to me that becoming a believer had suddenly wiped their pasts away as if with a magic wand.

I know God can do that, but I had never experienced that myself. My past still affected my life. As a believer I still needed healing. I wondered, *Have they ever dealt with their hurts? Are they just being good Christians? Oh, I know they are good! These ladies that I admire and respect are simply much stronger than I!* But now I saw these strong women touched by what I had just shared with them. And they began to minister to me in ways not too many people have been able to. One lady held my hands and prayed for me about something I had been begging God to do for a long time. I will never forget that evening with all those dear women surrounding me with such love and compassion, lifting me up to God in prayer. As I became vulnerable enough to let them pray for me things began to change.

But something else happened that week. Because I had shared that I was struggling in one area of my life and still had no answers, one evening during dinnertime, a precious lady quietly told me her story of similar struggles and how God was working in her life and her marriage. I had several questions and we shared our lives together. Then another older woman went to the room of one of our leaders, sat on the floor, and very timidly asked for prayer for wounds that she had been carrying for twenty years. She had occasionally shared her story, but had never truly revealed her heart. Now she was ready to open up and to receive healing also. I realized that my decision to be transparent had led to much healing—for me and for others.

I was in awe of God's goodness. I had expected judgment, or at best a discussion on how to reach other victims of child abuse. I had not expected to see women who seemingly "had it all together" in tears and seeking healing for their own brokenness. Here was God using my scars, while shattering the myth that missionaries are "superheroes" who always live perfect lives. I had just revealed my weakness and pain and God used it for His glory. He never forgets our scars; they are precious to Him. All I could do that week was hold out my hands, with gratefulness in my heart, to catch the blessings!

Ella's story lifts the shroud of silence and shame exposing one of the cruelest sins committed against our children. God wants our churches to be safe havens—healing places where the wounded, the sick, the broken, and the damaged can receive the "Balm of Gilead." Ella found that among her Project Hannah colleagues. I was amazed to once again witness the true nature of mercy. In the process of taking care of this "bruised reed" and lifting her up, we were also lifted to a new level of wholeness.

Chapter 6

. . . There is Strength!

"When you pass through the waters, I will be with you; And through the rivers, they will not overflow you. When you walk through the fire, you will not be scorched, Nor will the flame burn you."

—Isaiah 43:2

I had never before experienced anything like it! Streams of women dressed in exquisite attire consisting of almost every shade of red, yellow, orange, blue, green, and purple filled the church to overflowing. The harmonious voices, drums, dancing feet, and fervent prayers swelled upward in praise to God with a celebration that lasted more than four hours. I was overwhelmed with the glory of it all!

It seemed as though a "wind of fire" had filled this downtown church in Luanda—an absolute contrast to what one might expect to find in a war-torn country filled with so much suffering.

Watching their joyful faces, my soul was lifted up in praise and thanksgiving to God for the vibrant Project Hannah's prayer movement which counts more than 4,500 intercessors in such a needy place! I could not control the tears of thanksgiving that streamed down my cheeks. That night I wrote home, "Today, I saw *hope* dancing in Church!"

The Angolan Women's Affairs Minister, herself a *Women of Hope* listener, along with five other members of Parliament and other invited leaders, joined in the celebration. The next morning, at her invitation, we met in her office along with two other ministers. We discussed how we could work together to restore women's dignity and value through radio, prayer, and hands-on ministries. As our meeting ended I had the privilege of praying for each one of them as well as for the important work of helping the Angolan women find their

God-given destiny and potential. We all agreed that unless the government assures minimum respect and maximum opportunities, especially to women and children, Angola will continue to be depleted of its vitality and its most valuable resource.

Justina's story of indignity and restored vitality is a testament to God's hope winning over cultural and spiritual barriers. She carries deep scars from years of war, abuse, and godless traditions. But this story is also Hope's victory cry. After being refined by the fire of affliction, Justina has emerged as strong and purified as gold!

Being a woman here is not easy! Our value comes mostly from our strength to work hard in the fields and our ability to have babies. Our tradition entitles a man to be the "owner" of his daughters and wife. They must obey him without question. In my Ngaguela tribe, a woman is to be seen and used, but not heard. She remains a perpetual minor with no voice of her own. When a husband dies, his family is entitled to keep everything he owned, including the house. Nowadays, more educated families, and those living in the city, at least leave the house to the widow. But if she remarries, the house goes. She loses everything!

There are other traditions in my tribe that denigrate a woman's dignity. When a girl gets her first *kukula* (menstrual period) she is taken by older women to the *Chiso*—a mud hut in the forest, away from everyone. There she meets older women, the *Mambololo*, and others possessed by evil spirits. It is a very detailed and frightening ceremony. But mainly the *Mambololo* teaches her traditional dances, costumes related to marriage, how to live with the future husband's family, how to recognize spirit entities, and the secrets of the spirit world. She then vows never to tell anyone what she has learned, otherwise she will be cursed or even killed.

This automatically makes her fair game for marriage proposals, no matter how young she is or how underdeveloped her body might be. I thank God that my Christian parents never sent me to the *Chiso*, but I will never forget the day when they married me off to a supposedly "Christian" man. I was only fifteen years old and knew nothing about marriage or about my new husband-to-be. A few hours before my wedding ceremony, my mother told her sister to prepare me for what would happen and how I should behave on my wedding night. That night was the beginning of a nightmare that lasted for years!

The physical abuse, name-calling, cursing, and yelling began almost immediately. Once he tortured me so badly, I ended up at the ICU with a dangerous hemorrhage. I was three months pregnant. The baby survived, and on my way home I stopped at the police station and filed a complaint. I was terrified. They reluctantly listened, and filed the case—but that was all.

My husband would never spend even one penny on such a "worthless woman," as he used to call me. He never gave the children a single word of encouragement, counsel, a reprimand, or praise—nothing. The children were my "fault" and my responsibility. Forget the fact that I was a child myself! What did I know about raising children? But they kept coming—eight of them! My children grew up in a world filled with fear, hearing their father's constant threats that he was going to kill us all.

One day he pushed us all out of the house. *Where in the world will we go?* I wondered. We could not go to my parents because they lived in an area affected by war. For years I could not visit them—the crossfire was too dangerous. Who would take in nine of us! Even though I never wanted to see that man again I had no choice—we went back to the house and to my endless nightmare.

At the time, Angola was under the communist regime. My husband had become one of the party leaders in our village. He was already violent, but in this position he became even worse. His alcoholism got out of control, and the time he spent with other women, too. One day I found new clothes, for a woman and a baby, lying on the chair. I had just given birth to a baby girl so I assumed they were for us. I dressed myself and my baby in the new clothes. When he got home, he was furious and tore the clothes from both of us. They were not for us! My baby was left naked.

Then the war came to our village and we were moved to Luanda as war refugees. While there, I fell very ill. When we needed my husband the most he left us and went to live with one of his lovers in Bié. In Angolan culture, it is perfectly OK for a man to have more than one wife, so I was left alone to provide for my children. What else could I do? Even though I was sick I kept selling food on the streets as many poor people do in Luanda. When I look back on that time, I realize that only the true Christian values my parents taught me prevented me from sinning against God by going after other men, selling my body, or finding easier ways to get money.

During that time I started looking for a Christian church. I prayed and read the Bible, and God started to work in my heart. Meanwhile, my husband became diabetic and also tested HIV positive. That's when his lovers left him. So, abandoned, sick, and helpless he found his way back to us. Can you imagine my feelings when he showed up at my doorstep? I did not know what to say or how to feel! I ran inside. "Lord…after six years? What do I do with this man now? What should I say?" I felt God's hand on me, guiding me back to the door. He helped me talk with that man who had given me nothing but grief and pain for years!

He was so broken. His arrogance was gone. He listened quietly while I told him how I had found God. How He had changed me, taking away my anger and bitterness. And especially how I had found a group of Christian women through Project Hannah who gave me support and so much joy.

When he confessed his remorse for the terrible things he had done to us, I knew that the Holy Spirit had brought to his memory the things he learned years ago when he was a "Christian." After a long silence, I dared to ask him if he wanted to pray with me. And he did! He asked God to forgive his sins. He also asked for my forgiveness. And somehow God helped me to forgive that man whom I had prayed I would never see again in my life. That was God loving my enemy for me!

I wish I could say that we lived happily ever after, but no, there was never a good relationship between us. Life continued to be difficult, especially now with a sick man in the house. I needed God's strength, so I clung to His word. He used my Project Hannah friends to teach me the awesome power of prayer. They have encouraged me by teaching me that there is nothing greater than God's power to deliver us.

This was especially true during the most recent floods here in Luanda. In a matter of hours what little we had was washed away. With no sewage system in my neighborhood, the water rose and surrounded us with garbage, debris, and human feces. But in the midst of that terrible situation my Project Hannah friends came to help us. In word and in deed they taught me about the awesome power of prayer and that God's faithfulness, provision, and promises never fail.

My husband was dying; we were deep in debt and we had nothing left. But in the midst of it all I realized that my greatest need was not to get rid of my problems, but to hand them to God and let Him take control. The *Women of Hope* programs have helped me many times in my search for God, too. I did not have a radio, so I arranged to listen from my neighbor's house. Today I have my own radio and never miss one program because it truly helps women like me—whether they are alone in small villages or on crowded big city streets.

I remember that, "The effective prayer of a righteous man [or woman] can accomplish much," (James 5:16). I have seen the truth of these words not just in my own life, but also in our government and society. Their attitude is changing! Finally women are receiving recognition not for what they produce or do, but for who they are. God is also answering my Project Hannah friends' prayers for us.

As my faith grew, God's grace and power intervened, and things started to change! First it was my husband's heart. Whenever he was well enough to work, he would bring home whatever he received to pay the bills. He did that until he passed away. I was grateful. Then my salary increased five-fold. My two unemployed children got jobs. All my children now attend school. I have a good church family that loves us and cares for us. My church leaders trust me and encourage me to continue growing in my faith.

Amazing! Who would have thought that this "worthless woman"—as her husband used to call her—would become the Church Women's Ministry Leader of her denomination for the whole province? "I do the best I can to please my Lord who saved me!" Justina says with a grateful smile. "My greatest prayer, however, is yet to be answered—to see my four unsaved children coming to God and receiving the hope and strength He gives us. Only then they will know the joy of the Lord which indeed, is my strength."

Chapter 7

. . . There is Freedom!

"So if the Son makes you free,

you will be free indeed."

—John 8:36

When God called me to start Project Hannah, He never gave me a strategic plan—a business plan. I remember struggling to explain it to my leaders. They wanted to see something, but I had nothing to show them. I understood their concerns, but this was a "God thing" and not really my idea at all! But God worked on their hearts and they cautiously allowed me to walk by faith.

At the time, my husband was the only one that believed with me. He had seen the anguish, the sleepless nights in prayer, and what he called my "insane obedience." I could not get away from God's call. Beginning with one weekly radio program and a group of twelve Chinese women praying with me in Singapore, gradually God revealed to me His strategic plan. Oswald Chambers' words best describe God's strategy for Project Hannah, "Pray not for greater works. Prayer is the greater work!"

The "greater work" done by Project Hannah intercessors in more than 105 countries is opening prison doors and taking Jesus' hope and freedom to men and women in jails in Europe, Asia, Africa, and South America. When I was first invited by TWR Paraguay to establish Project Hannah's ministry there, I was taken to visit a jail in old downtown Asunción. Ever since, I have seen true hope in Christ winning the battle for the hearts and minds of the dear women locked in that jail.

According to a UN report, there are more female prisoners per capita in Paraguay, a country nestled between Bolivia, Argentina, and Brazil, than in any other country in the world. In fact, three times the world average! Paraguay serves as a corridor for the trafficking of stolen cars, drugs, and prostitutes. Authorities are busy cracking down on drug cartels and arresting traffickers, many of whom are Paraguayan women, as well as women from neighboring countries. This explains the disproportionate number of female inmates in Paraguay.

Once a week, a Project Hannah team of volunteers offers hope and mercy to more than 200 prisoners and 25 children crammed into a prison built to house only 120 at *Carcere Buen Pastor* (Good Shepherd Prison). They tend to the physical and spiritual needs of the inmates, who are often unloved and forgotten by their own families.

Through one-on-one and group prayer time, the prisoners are taught about the power of prayer.

Their minds are being renewed through study of the Bible and other Christian literature. Their old thinking patterns are being exchanged with biblical truths. The inmates are learning to trust God . . . even in a place where no one can be trusted!

Hope's triumph in this dark place is seen in the lives of women who used to live in despair and filth, who cursed and called each other terrible names, and who now sing together in a choir, begun by one of the Project Hannah volunteers. Every week, sweet, beautiful praise music echoes throughout the high walls of that awful place. It is truly amazing!

The stories are many—today there is a church of about 100 members at *Buen Pastor*, and Ramona is one of them. Jesus, the great liberator of the oppressed, brought her out of despair. Even though imprisoned, Ramona lives free in the radiance of His light and in the power of His hope!

My husband looked at me and said, "I am leaving." And he left—just like that—and moved in with his lover. My heart was stabbed with rejection and I kept asking myself in disbelief, *How could he do this to us?* That was the beginning of a long, hard road for me. After a month without being able to pay the rent, I was forced to leave the house. I had no job and no place to go with my five children. For weeks I searched for a job—any job—that would help me make ends meet in order to survive, but it was hopeless. Who would take in a woman with five children?

One day I happened to run into a woman who, after listening to my story, offered me a job and a place to stay . . . just a small house behind hers with a few pieces of furniture. I could not believe it. Finally here was light at the end of the tunnel! I was ecstatic, and even though I did not know this woman, I gladly accepted her offer.

However, it did not take long for me to realize that her generosity had strings attached. She was deeply involved in illegal activities and I was caught in the middle of it all. I knew I was in serious trouble.

When she realized I had figured it out, she confronted me and threatened me, saying that if I ever tried to get away, I would forever regret what would happen to one of my children. I was trapped and scared wondering what would happen to me. Two months went by and all I could think about was how to get away! I could not sleep . . . I was terrified!

One morning, a police drug squad vehicle stopped outside the house. They came around the back, knocked at my door and asked all kinds of questions. I explained that I simply lived there with my children and worked for her. I had nothing to do with her business. They pushed me around and treated me as though I were a criminal. Thankfully, one of them ordered the others to leave me alone and not hurt me. Since I was not the person they were looking for, they left—or so I thought.

A few minutes later they broke down my employer's front door. Sure enough, inside they found a large quantity of cocaine of the highest value. Then they returned to my house and accused me of being a drug dealer also. In spite of my fear in the midst of that terrible situation, I felt calm. Even when they took my children from me and I was facing prison—a high price to pay—I felt a strange sense of relief, for we would all finally be freed from this evil woman.

I was put behind bars and told to wait for my trial. When they gave me a special cell, bigger than the others and with more light, I wondered why? Now I know—it was God watching over me. After six months of waiting, the day of the trial came and I was sentenced to five years in prison without parole!

Now, I am so thankful that Pastor Jaime came regularly to the prison to talk to us about God. I remember the day I finally understood what he said about God's love for me. That was the very first time I heard about Jesus and what He did for me on the cross. How could He die for me—an abandoned, rejected woman thrown into this crowded jail? The thought just blew my mind!

I had hungered for love, acceptance, and peace for so long, so I asked Pastor Jaime to pray with me. That day he led me to Jesus. I confessed my sins and asked God to forgive me . . . and He did. He forgave every one of my sins right then and there! He also miraculously healed the pain in my heart and I felt a tremendous sense of freedom. Yes, I am still in prison, but my heart has been set free! This experience enabled me to crawl out of my long, dark tunnel of loneliness, unbelief, and fear—to a place of light, faith, peace, and even joy.

I know now that God was taking care of me all along. He sent that policeman to protect me. He also took care of my children when they were taken away from me. Life in jail is never easy but time and time again He has protected me in terrible circumstances in this tough place! There are many struggles and dangers, but Jesus has always kept me safe.

Now I get up every day at 5 a.m. to pray. I also enjoy a good relationship with all the other inmates because Jesus walks with me here. He helps me to share His love by comforting them, counseling them in their troubles, and even praying with them. And God has answered my prayers, providing every one of my needs. He even gave me a job working with the guards. Unbelievable! I can now support my children as family and friends take care of them.

When I think about that woman who hurt my children and me so badly, God helps me to pray that somehow, someday she will meet Jesus too, and be saved and forgiven as I have been. Although I am paying for somebody else's crime, my situation helps me to understand Jesus' sacrifice for me. My reward is that I have met Jesus here!

Every week, when the Project Hannah ladies come to visit us it is like a party. We love those women! And we know they love us too with their encouragement and practical gifts. But, best of all we love the music and the Word of God. Many tough, hardened women have been changed as they have accepted Jesus into their hearts through this ministry. What a miracle!

As for me, I have become a happy woman! I am thankful for everyone who has helped me, especially the Project Hannah volunteers—they are truly rays of light in this dark place. But most of all, my greatest thanks goes to God for sending Jesus to pay my debt and set me free. Like He said—I am free indeed!

Project Hannah's team in Paraguay has been anointed "to bind up the brokenhearted, to proclaim freedom for the captives and release from darkness for the prisoners," (Isaiah 61:1 NIV). Ramona's story reminds me of another prisoner who wrote to Christian believers in Philippi, "Rejoice in the Lord always; again I will say rejoice!" (Philippians 4:4). Paul, like Ramona, was imprisoned unjustly. And Ramona, like the great apostle, makes the choice daily to rejoice in spite of it all. In the process, God makes her soul fly free, soaring like an eagle in the sky!

Chapter 8

. . . There is Redemption!

"...THEY WILL BE CALLED OAKS OF RIGHTEOUSNESS, A PLANTING OF THE LORD FOR THE DISPLAY OF HIS SPLENDOR."

—ISAIAH 61:3 NIV

With her musician husband, beautiful voice, guitar, and her amazing story, Marlene de Fatima Vasques promotes Project Hannah's ministry and Jesus' life-changing message of hope all over Brazil. As I listened to her, I was transported to a theater of war between good and evil, despair and hope, darkness and light. Hope's victory came through the power of God's redemption in her life, equipping her to minister to women in ways few of us can.

My father was nineteen and my mother seventeen when they married. My mother was a beautiful woman with black shiny hair, big dark eyes, and soft skin. She was a great communicator and taught us many good things. My father was handsome and always smartly dressed and well-groomed. I got my love for music and singing from him. They were a striking couple with an enviable marriage.

I am the oldest of four girls. I was especially loved and spoiled by my parents, grandparents, uncles, and aunts. I was the "star" of the family. At eight, I learned Spanish and started to sing Mexican songs in a popular children's TV musical. Every week, until I was fourteen, my father would take me to the city on his motorcycle to sing in this TV musical. My mother used to sew beautiful Mexican clothes with colorful embroidery for me. Wearing them I looked like an authentic Mexican girl. My family dreamed that I would become famous throughout

Brazil. They all supported my career. We were a happy family—my parents, my sisters, and I.

But my father's job kept him away from home for days at a time. And even though they truly loved each other, both my parents fell into adultery. I never understood why. First my father . . . and then my mother. They remained together for a few months and my father continued to provide for our needs and to respect my mother. I never heard him raise his voice to her, but life was never the same in our home again.

At this time my mother started selling clothes in the neighboring cities. She wanted to prove that she was able to make it without him. While both were away a dear aunt took care of us girls. But my sisters and I were very hurt by these drastic changes. My joy was gone and so was my trust. A nagging thought kept rattling in my brain, "Why live anymore?" I just wanted to die. So, I wrote a letter to my parents saying that it wasn't their fault and then swallowed a bottle of 20 pills. After I took the pills, I went out on the street. All I remember is waking up in the hospital. My father happened to be in town that day, so he brought me home. I had crossed the bridge over the abyss of life. That near-death experience not only took away my fears, but also catapulted me into something worse—the world of drugs.

When my father decided to move thousands of miles away to Santarem, a city at the mouth of the Amazon, my mother moved us to Brasilia, the capital city. But big-city life, where drugs flowed freely, was bad news for a young addict like me.

My mother was too hurt, too proud to accept anything from my father, even money for groceries. Poverty engulfed us and we ended up living in the slums, never quite sure where our next meal would come from.

Eventually, my mother found a job at a night bar where she also started selling her body—servicing up to thirty men a night. Soon she became a pimp. She drowned her pain in alcohol and became deeply involved with witchcraft, bringing those evil spirits home with her. Life literally became hell for my sisters and me.

One terrible day, she and another prostitute friend staggered home at daybreak. "Is this a time for a mother to arrive home?" I confronted her. Drunk as she was, she grabbed me by the throat and began to strangle me. Her prostitute friend came to my rescue, pulling her away from me. She screamed, "Run Marlene, run!" I spent the whole day huddled in the woods, afraid to go home. I waited until she left the house for "work" that evening and crept back inside. The next day she didn't remember a thing.

I just wanted to get away, so I rarely slept at home anymore. I was often invited to sing at different events. On one occasion I became acquainted with a couple—two of the biggest drug traffickers in town—

who gave me my first joint of marijuana. I told myself I wasn't ever going to try it again, I just wanted to experience this "magical world" they talked about. Of course, I got hooked and became their "little trophy"—a popular rock star and singer, and the youngest marijuana consumer in town. Through them I came to know several powerful drug dealers who freely provided me with all the "substance" I needed. But within two years they had all died—some were murdered, others died of AIDS.

I hated my mother's promiscuity, yet I soon found myself following her footsteps. I started a job as a crooner, singing at bars and nightclubs, and wore sensual clothes to attract the attention I craved. I paid dearly for that attention—often suffering sexual violence. I recall at least four times when God freed me from the powerful grip of dangerous men. Each time I thought I was going to die, but now I know it was God's hand of love that reached down into the pit and rescued me.

My sensitive little eight-year-old sister, Adalgiza, was very traumatized by the events happening in our family. Every day she would look at a poster of Jesus I had bought and hung next to my bed, kneel down and in tears she would pray for that man in the picture to bring my parents together again. It was heartbreaking to see her cry that way.

Adalgiza did not know who she was praying to, but Jesus heard my little sister's prayer! Later, after we both became Christians, she told me, "I made a promise to pray every day until He brought our parents together again." At the end of that year, I received a letter from my father telling me how much he missed my mother and his four girls and how he still loved all of us. He also wrote to my mother and to my second sister. He wanted all of us to come back home again. So, we did.

We were all living under one roof again, but in reality we were worlds apart—my mother an alcoholic, my sister and I drug addicts, and my younger sisters were severely-damaged emotionally. My father suffered much seeing his beautiful daughters in that miserable state and his wife a total stranger. Nonetheless, we pretended everything was all right and that we were a big, happy family again. But we were broken; our souls were desperately sick. Only God could heal us now.

And healing came in the most unexpected way. While singing at a nightclub, I met Wesley, another professional nightclub singer. One day he offered to take me home. During the ride I started to talk about Jesus' return. (I had found a Bible in our house and used to carry it in my backpack for my "protection," and I liked to read about Jesus in the book of Revelation.) One day I told Wesley that Jesus was going to come back. Surprised, he looked at me and said, "If Jesus comes back He will be killed again." Smiling I answered him, "You are crazy! He is going to return with power and great glory. Not like a man, but as God."

From that day on, besides music, we had a common interest: the Bible. Wesley would come to my house every day, and for six months we read and discussed Scripture together, especially the mysterious book of Revelation. Gradually we became conscious that we both needed to make changes. He needed to abandon alcohol, and I, the drugs. We knew that we were slowly being destroyed by them. We tried to stop a couple of times, but to no avail. Then one of my aunts told us, "You should go to church since you spend so much time reading this Bible." Interestingly enough she was not even a Christian! So, we agreed, and she introduced us to an evangelical church! This was the beginning of our new life.

One Wednesday night, Wesley, with his enormous "black power" hair, and I, dressed as a hippie, stopped off at a bar before we went to church. He had two glasses of beer and I had my drugs. But that night none of it "worked!" So we went to church, where God was waiting for us.

We sat in the front pew as Pastor Aristótens started the service, "Brothers and sisters, today we are going to start our Bible study on the book of Revelation!" *Revelation?* We couldn't believe our ears! From that point on we were drawn to that place. For two months we attended Wednesday night Bible studies on Revelation, never missing a single one.

When Pastor Aristótens found out Wesley and I were musicians, he invited us to sing at the Sunday worship service. He knew I had composed a song called "Maranatha." It was my very first song—one that Jesus gave me even before I met Him! We agreed, but when we arrived at the church on Sunday, people avoided looking at us. The pastor was in big trouble! How dare he invite two worldly musicians—an alcoholic and a drug addict—to participate in the service? Who would do such a thing?

But that compassionate and courageous man did, and we sang. Since we Brazilians have a passion for music, our song quickly won the hearts of the entire congregation!

Pastor Aristótens then preached an evangelistic message complete with an altar call. In tears, Wesley and I both fell on our knees, publicly receiving Jesus as our Savior. All my sins started to pass through my mind like a movie. I wept and wept. At the end of the service, he said to us, "Get ready to give your testimonies next Sunday. Tell them what God is doing in your lives." We were eager to do so, and since that Sunday we have never ceased telling our story.

We went to a recovery program for the next few months and along with our sins, Jesus also cleansed us from our addictions! After some time, I invited one of my friends—a major drug dealer—to attend a service in which we were going to give our testimonies. He sat in the front pew and listened closely to each word we said. Before we even finished speaking, he started to cry aloud saying, "I want this God of Wesley and Marlene!" He fell on his knees and gave his life completely to Jesus. That was the first soul won to the Lord by our testimony. After staying in a rehabilitation facility for only two months he came out totally clean. Later he attended seminary, and today he is a pastor and a church planter in South Brazil.

Thankfully, my family saw the miraculous transformation when I became clean and my whole life changed before their eyes. My two younger sisters were the first ones to come to church with us and to accept healing for their wounded souls. Today they are godly women of faith and integrity. My little sister Adalgiza became a "praying Hannah." She now leads a prayer group and is one of the greatest intercessors I have ever known. She travels on her knees with me as we go around Brazil presenting the Project Hannah ministry.

I've lost count of how many members of my large, extended family have come to Christ. My other sister continued to use drugs for another ten years but lived a seemingly-normal life, even while attending University. Then she had a powerful encounter with Jesus. She left the drugs, and her life was changed forever. Today she is a well-respected lawyer.

After my father became a believer, he and my mother had a few years of happiness together even though she had not found new life with Jesus. When my father was fifty-three, he called me and told me that he was a man "completely transformed by the Holy Spirit of God." One month later, he died from a massive heart attack.

My mother only came to faith many years later. It was a very long and difficult process. Satan didn't want to let go of her. She had terrible episodes of demon possession that almost killed her. However, God used my father's death to complete His work of freedom in my mother's life. Adalgiza, the great intercessor, also had many prayer groups praying and fasting for our mother's salvation until God saved her—delivering her from addiction at the same time.

Today my mother is a woman of prayer who loves God and loves to witness to women who are where she used to be. God in His miraculous mercy has given us the grace to forgive each other and to deal with the hurts and wounds of the past. At 70, she is a restored and beautiful woman. Through the years my mother has brought several of her prostitute friends to Jesus. Fearlessly she goes into the ghetto and witnesses to them, counseling both the young and the old.

After seventeen years ministering with a Christian band, my husband Wesley and I were invited to join Trans World Radio (TWR) Brazil to introduce the ministry while performing in churches, listener rallies, conferences, and through the media.

I fell in love with Project Hannah the first time I heard about it. Its prayer movement is very dear to my heart. It is a simple but wonderful concept—a wave of prayer circling the globe 24/7. Project Hannah is truly a "project of love" to me. I asked God to pour out His compassion in my heart in double measure so I could better serve the women wherever He sent me. He has granted my request in ways I could never imagine.

Isaiah 61:3 has been fulfilled in my life. When I look back to where I came from—drugs, prostitution, witchcraft, misery, hopelessness—and then I look forward and see the blessing of God flowing through my life, I am overwhelmed. This is the reason why I cannot stop telling my story, especially to women who are lost as I was. When I tell them how God literally snatched me out of hell, they can't resist His grace.

Chapter 9

. . . There is Wisdom!

"THOSE WHO HAVE INSIGHT WILL SHINE BRIGHTLY LIKE THE BRIGHTNESS OF THE EXPANSE OF HEAVEN, AND THOSE WHO LEAD THE MANY TO RIGHTEOUSNESS, LIKE THE STARS FOREVER AND EVER."

—DANIEL 12:3

Buakab Ronghanam's graceful movements and petite stature is typical of the beautiful women of Thailand. However, there is nothing small about her! She is a great visionary and leader whose passion for God and compassion for people are limitless! Dr. Buakab has led Project Hannah's ministry in Thailand for over a decade. Hope and faith in God have sustained her through the years on her painful journey from an obscure Thai village to a place of international recognition. In the process, she has brought many to faith in our Lord Jesus.

Like most little Thai girls, I could curl my fingers backward, moving my cupped hands and bent knees in slow, fluid motion to the sound of the music—I love traditional Thai dance! And like the dance, my life was lived in seemingly "slow motion" in a small village in Nakornphanom Province, close to the Laotian border. My father, a schoolteacher and a deacon in a Buddhist temple, was my hero. My mother was a medium. I remember dreaming of being a helpful teacher like my father and a good woman, assisting the poor and healing the sick, like my mother.

The Maekong River, flowing peacefully all year round, mirrored the serenity in the hearts of the Thai people until the Vietnamese War broke out in 1965. I was only eleven years old. At that time, another kind of war broke out in my family, destroying my parents' marriage. My heart was broken! My mother remarried, and when I was thirteen, my stepfather told my mother to pull me out of school. My dreams of being a great teacher were shattered, and I lost hope. Now, without a purpose for living, for weeks I looked for a way to end my life.

Over the years, things went from bad to worse in our family. My eldest brother became a gangster and life as we knew it was gone. But God was watching over me and my siblings in order to fulfill His plans in and through us. One day He sent someone to tell my brother about Jesus, leading him to a new life. After he accepted Jesus, he left the gang and his old lifestyle. He was a changed man!

He began to attend church and invited me to study English there with an Australian missionary. Finally I was able to be in a classroom again! After my lesson I went to the worship service and heard for the first time about the true and living God, the One who lovingly created everything—including me! I remember praying for one thing, "God, if you are real . . . and a loving God, as they say you are, please help me further my studies, then I will give the rest of my life to You."

God answered my prayer in a miraculous way. My brother won an American Field Service Scholarship to study in America. But he decided not to go. Instead he got a job as an English teacher at a private school in Korat, near Bangkok. He was only nineteen, yet he offered to take all four of us children with him! That's how much God's love had changed him. We each received a scholarship, which helped him to care for us without having to pay school fees.

I followed my brother to church every Sunday for the next three years. During that time, God answered my many prayers, but I didn't really surrender my life to Jesus. Then one night, when I was sixteen, the Holy Spirit convicted me of my sin and I humbly received Christ into my life. I felt that same great joy that I saw in my brother. It was the first time, since my parents' divorce, that I had felt free and fully provided for, lacking nothing.

God began to speak to me. One day at a youth retreat, I felt God telling me that I would be "His mouthpiece" to warn my Thai people of their sins. I did not fully understand what God wanted from me, but my rationale was that if Jesus gave His all for me, how could I give less than my all for Him? Besides, when God answered my prayer asking for further schooling, had I not promised that I would serve Him with all my life? It was a promise I intended to keep.

I studied to become an accountant and later worked in Christian media, producing programs for children and youth. Next I received a scholarship to study at the Sydney Missionary and Bible College (SMBC), in Australia. From then on I felt as if I was on "God's conveyer belt," serving in several different Christian ministries and teaching over radio, TV, and the Christian press. My childhood dream was being fulfilled.

But life is not a "bed of roses" is it? We cannot avoid the thorns—and they hurt! I know because as time went on, I was hurt by life's thorns in ways a woman should never be!

Thailand is a land of rich cultural heritage. Christian missionaries have been serving here for nearly 200 years, yet 95 percent of my people still follow Buddhism. Our society is going through visceral changes brought on by the Internet and other modern media. It has invaded our homes with materialism, changing our values and culture . . . ripping our country apart. Yet one thing has remained the same—the ancient Thai practice of a husband having multiple wives. It is against God's law. It is also against Thai laws, but men from every social level practice it here and their wives suffer greatly. If a wife leaves that situation she is automatically branded as "not good enough," or that there is "something wrong with her."

I know about the stigma and suffering, because I am one of those wives. At 23 I married a handsome soldier. He was my age and a new Christian believer. Our happiness was complete when God gave us two wonderful children. When our daughter and son were ages seven and eight, my husband fell in love with a university student 10 years younger than me. I will never forget the day he asked me to take his lover into our home. I just couldn't do it. It was against everything I stood for as a wife, mother, and Christian leader. So he sent us away. That was the end of my beautiful marriage and family life. My perfect little world had crumbled again!

Ten painful years went by. When my children went abroad to college, I applied for a full scholarship from the Theological Center for Asia in Singapore to complete a Master of Cross-Cultural Studies and a

Master of Divinity. My family may have been pulled apart and my heart broken, but my faith remained intact. I clung to the promise God gave me, that I would be His mouthpiece to my people. This was my chance to prepare myself to serve others! I drank deeply from God's word, spending hours at His feet. In turn, He touched every fiber of my being with His love and compassion. He inspired me to use any free time I had to go out and share God's love with my Thai people working in construction sites all over Singapore. Serving others accelerated the healing in my heart and soul.

When I returned home to Thailand, I realized that despite my passion for study, the degrees I had received were not my greatest accomplishment. The lessons in savoring Jesus' intimacy, the tests I had passed in living for Him and serving Him in a foreign land, the many lives changed by Christ—those were my glory! My life was meaningful again, and I had tasted how ". . .in all things God works for the good of those who love Him . . ." (Roman 8:28 NIV).

I realized also that Thai society—which traditionally values women only as housekeepers and child bearers—had changed much. Now there are many women in high positions of leadership in the government, as well as in the business world.

This is not the case, however, among the Thai Christian community despite many women having higher education qualifications and the skills and gifting for ministry. My marital status is also a stumbling block for some. Even though I have never remarried, I carry this stigma with me. However, the people who know me respect and fully support me in everything they see me doing for the Lord. I am blessed.

After thirty years' teaching like my father, I wondered when God would bring to pass my dream of tending to the poor and needy, like my mother. But He never does anything halfway, does He? When I turned fifty, He inspired me to set up a foundation called For Better Life. Through it, we have built five homes for poor, abused, and orphaned children, one primary school, four tribal Christian villages for homeless families in our city and by His grace we have planted nine tribal churches!

For more than a decade God has brought another great blessing into my life. As the director of "Voice of Peace," a Christian media organization, I was invited to attend a TWR Radio Producers Conference in Singapore where a new ministry for women was being introduced. I was excited about going because women's ministry was, and still is, my passion. I was impressed to learn how God called Marli Spieker, how He gave her the vision and the right strategy to respond to the cries of suffering women worldwide. God had carved that same vision in my heart and I understood that Project Hannah was the perfect tool to help fulfill that vision of reaching out to my Thai sisters. Here was one more opportunity to be "God's mouthpiece."

The Project Hannah leadership invited me to take the position of Project Hannah National Coordinator establishing a partnership with Voice of Peace. I was thrilled! I committed myself to developing Project Hannah in Thailand, producing radio programs, setting up prayer groups and interceding for Thai women as well as women around the world. What a great opportunity for my people!

Today *Women of Hope* programs are broadcast from more than twenty-four community radio stations and even twelve major stations belonging to our Buddhist government, covering the whole of Thailand and neighboring countries. Scores of women and men listening to the programs have turned to Christ.

One of the greatest joys I have had as "God's mouthpiece" over the radio, is to learn of a man called

Khun Somwang Kongkeaw, an ex-convict at Udorn Prison in Thailand. Somwang is not proud of many things in his past. He broke the law of the land, and he broke God's law in ways he does not like even to remember. Rotting in his cell one day, he turned on the radio and heard me speaking on *Women of Hope*. He thought, *This is for women—not for tough guys like me!* But he was strangely drawn to what I was saying. He listened to the whole program and jotted down the contact address at the end.

Then he wrote to us, "Today I listened to your *Women of Hope*. I heard your message and I understood it. You asked if I wanted to change my life and have my sins forgiven. I do not know God, but I prayed with you to accept your Jesus into my life. I want to be a new person. When I prayed, I felt something in my heart that I have never felt before. I think it is the love of this God you told me about."

Not long after his decision to follow Christ, Somwang fell seriously ill and was taken to a nearby hospital. He was in so much pain he could not fall asleep. He tossed and turned without any relief. Suddenly he saw a bright light approaching his bedside. There stood a figure in a bright white robe. He heard a clear voice, "Do you want to be healed?" In fear he answered, "I do. Yes I do." Then the second question, "And do you believe that I can heal you?"

Somwang was raised in Buddhism and knew very little about the power of the one true God. But, at that moment, he connected that figure with the same Jesus, the Son of a Living God, who he had heard about on *Women of Hope!* "Yes, Jesus," he said softly, "I believe!" A few minutes later he fell into a deep sleep that lasted until late the next morning. When he awoke the pain was completely gone—he was well again! The doctors could not explain what had happened, but they released him to go back to prison.

Now he had to tell his friends. Some did not believe him, but others did. He kept telling them that the man who healed him was Jesus. He explained to them who Jesus is—the Son of the living God who came to save the world, forgive our sins, and set us free! What a message for an audience craving freedom with every breath!

Listening to him, many who were sick asked him to pray for them. God in His mercy honored Somwang's faith and many were miraculously healed. He kept listening to *Women of Hope* and reported to us what God was doing. He wanted to know more about Jesus, so we sent him our Bible correspondence course. His friends also wanted to study so he sent us a list of their names. A miracle unfolded right before our eyes! His life-changing experience attracted more than 100 prisoners who completed the Bible course in the first year.

But that's not all! Somwang's changed life also inspired the prison officials and through his testimony four of them accepted Christ. Because of his transformation and excellent behavior they made him the overseer of other prisoners. This promotion gave him an even greater platform to witness to all the prisoners. During the five years after listening to *Women of Hope* for the first time, Somwang had led more than 2,000 prisoners to study the Word of God! More than 700 of them accepted Christ and were baptized.

The director even gave him permission to build a chapel inside the prison. This was dedicated with a baptismal service of 140 prisoners, both male and female, a tremendous testimony of God's greatness and the true freedom He gives to His beloved children. I wish you could have seen their radiant faces!

Then the day came when Somwang's time was up and he was set free. However, his heart was with his new spiritual family in that jail. So he received permission to continue teaching weekly Bible Lessons to about 200 men and women inside that place of painful memories. It is mind-boggling! Who could have imagined that a radio program, written by women for women, would touch a rough convict's heart, thereby planting a church of more than 200 members in the heart of a high security prison in a Buddhist country?

But the story does not end there! Inspired by Somwang's testimony we have set up a weekly Bible study program and offered inmates in 45 other prisons the opportunity to take part in the Bible correspondence course! Among other things, we recently distributed one thousand gospel books, adding to the nearly 30,000 that have been sent into prisons throughout Thailand.

I am thankful for God's sons and daughters who, with me, are being used as "God's mouthpieces," proclaiming freedom in Christ to lost and forgotten souls across our beloved country. The Spirit of God through His Word, which "never comes back void," continues to soften hardened criminals' hearts to receive Him.

Such is the God we serve! Never did I dare to dream that He would use me—a broken, stigmatized woman—to "bind up the brokenhearted" around me. I marvel to see His faithfulness; helping me to teach simple men and women, and even international Christian leaders, as a volunteer professor at Haggai Institute. It is very humbling to see God still using me to bring His hope and unconditional love to those in great need of it.

I think my mother and father would love to see their reflection, purified by Jesus' identity, in their little girl. God in His mercy fulfilled all my girlhood dreams. He is my "Dream Giver." He continues to enlarge my soul with His passion to see multitudes of Thai people freed from the bondage of sin and bowing down, not just before our good Thai King, but before the King of Kings! My Jesus.

Chapter 10

. . . There is Infinite Mercy!

"BUT TO THE DEGREE THAT YOU SHARE THE SUFFERINGS OF CHRIST, KEEP ON REJOICING, SO THAT ALSO AT THE REVELATION OF HIS GLORY YOU MAY REJOICE WITH EXULTATION."

—1 PETER 4:13

The last story I want to share with you is a deeply personal one I experienced during a season of great sorrow in my life. It was a time when God caused me to walk through the valley of the shadow of death, one of the most depressing and terrifying places I had ever been. A time when I was served and blessed by those I had gone to serve and bless. A time when I learned one precious lesson I hope never to forget . . . that when we lift others, we are lifted as well. This is all in the nature of mercy and this is the holy exchange that keeps us humble.

I was still grieving the death of my dear mother, as well as that of our strong, handsome, and godly 28-year-old son who had died a sudden, accidental death, when I received yet another chilling phone call. Our oldest son Marcio's family had been in a near-fatal car accident. The news sent shock waves to the depths of my soul. Subconsciously I held my hand on my heart, afraid that once more one of its broken pieces would be yanked out of my chest . . . and I pled for God's mercy.

Our two grandsons were flown to a trauma center by helicopter. Steffan, our athletic boy, had a fractured vertebra and torn ligaments. Just five years old, Logan suffered severe head injuries and bleeding deep in his brain that was inoperable. His face and forehead were completely ripped open. Doctors predicted that if he recovered, he would have significant brain damage, with paralysis in his left side, requiring extensive physical therapy.

In my mind I knew that circumstances out of our control are the perfect backdrop for the displaying of God's power. In my heart, though, like a wounded mama bear, I fought to hold them close as if pushing them back into my own flesh. The pain threw me into my Father's arms and His Word started flooding my mind. "*For He will give His angels charge concerning you, to guard you in all your ways. They will bear you up in their hands, that you do not strike your foot against a stone. . . He will call upon Me, and I will answer him; I will be with him in trouble; I will rescue him and honor him,*" (Psalm 91:11-12, 15).

How many times had I broadcast these same words to women all over the world? Often I had seen God miraculously rescue women from the most oppressive situations. Time after time I had witnessed how our effort to seek biblical justice through prayer, speak truth into their lives over the radio and Internet, and powerfully introduce Christ at the point of their felt needs was accomplishing a worldwide work of redemption. In so many cultures I had seen the powerful change in women's lives—from fear and hopelessness to a life of dignity and joy! Nothing but the power of God released by the prayer of His people could do that.

These few stories in this simple book are but a small glimpse of hope's overwhelming victory of forgiveness, salvation, and healing. That is the consuming passion and certainty of my life. And yet . . . at that moment, alone in my kitchen, I was pushed back to the valley of the shadow of death. I needed someone to remind me of all of that. That God's hope is the ultimate winner! In His hope there are no losers. In His economy, even to die is gain! At that moment I was in the same place of suffering as my sisters in Cambodia, the Amazon jungles, in the long, dark winter of the soul of many Scandinavian women. Indeed, pain is universal. But so is hope!

And it was that hope that brought my mind to God's miraculous power set in motion by the corporate, earnest prayer I had witnessed since Project Hannah's first prayer meeting back in 1997. Today, that single prayer meeting has grown to a prayer movement that has spread through more than 100 countries. So, I reached out to my own and sent an email to Project Hannah's intercessors asking them specifically to "pray that God would send His angels to touch and heal our boys." Like wildfire, prayer was ignited worldwide. And at that moment, my family became a recipient of Project Hannah's worldwide ministry of prayer. Amongst the hundreds of emails we received there was one from a Paraguayan women's jail, "We are praying for your family. God *will* send His angels to touch and heal the boys."

That email took me back to my first visit in that crammed, dirty, smelly, dark jail with broken walls covered with cobwebs. Worse yet was the spiritual oppression in the air. When asked to speak to the whole group I began, "We are all fellow offenders! We all have broken God's law, and we all deserve the death penalty. But Jesus came to pay our debt in full and to set us free." They responded, understanding that eternal freedom and salvation were free—if they just believed in Jesus and asked him into their hearts. Weeping, confessing their sins, and crying aloud to God in repentance, many surrendered their lives to Jesus. I have never seen such brokenness. We were in the midst of a miracle among miracles!

A year later I went back and saw a total transformation. The broken walls covered with cobwebs were now clean and painted pink! The prisoners' faces were radiant, their lives transformed. Many had become Project Hannah intercessors. Now in their simple newfound faith they reasoned that if God could forgive their awful pasts and heal their broken souls, healing our boys' bodies was just a small task for Him.

Back in Pennsylvania, after Logan had spent two days in a coma, the miracle happened. Five days after the accident, after thorough evaluation, he walked out of that hospital with his sparkling personality intact, his face all patched up with over 300 stitches, but with no need for any therapy at all. The trauma doctor could only shake his head and say, "Amazing!" None of the doctors' predictions for Logan ever came to pass! His big brother too, left without any residual side effects from the accident.

Two weeks later, at bed time Logan asked God to send "angels to protect our family." He had never prayed that way before, so his mom asked him if he had ever seen an angel. "Yes, at the hospital," he answered matter-of-factly. Then he started describing them in great detail. "They were *humongous* pretty angels, Mom! They were helping the doctors make me better." He also said that they touched his body everywhere he had been injured. Michelle, his mom, asked, "How many angels were there?" He paused for a moment and said, "I don't know . . . there were too many. I couldn't count them! But they were singing for me!"

Science cannot explain what happened, but my faith can! It was the power of prayer and hope. It was God answering the prayers of many, including those forgotten women locked away in a prison in Paraguay. They had knelt on that cold jail's cement floor and in faith summoned God's angels into Logan's ICU room thousands of miles away. And in His mercy, He honored their faith.

The Bible says, "In the day of my trouble I shall call upon You, for You will answer me," (Psalm 86:7). Those "criminals" ministered joy and hope to my family, upholding us at a time when our faith was shaken to the core. At that moment, the "Angel of His Presence" touched not only Logan's little body, but all of us in our places of brokenness—physical, emotional, and spiritual.

The women we serve have taught me many precious lessons. Listening to their stories I often feel I am standing on "holy ground." Their pain is immensely greater than mine. Their presence, impregnated with God's sustaining power and hope, inspires me to keep faithful to God's calling in my life. To never give up. To stand the test. To embrace courage. To dare to believe in the impossible. To endure the unendurable—that's when only God's grace will do. They personify Bill Hybels' description of endurance, "Endurance sustains courage . . . gives sustaining power to discipline . . . turns our vision into reality. If you are walking with God, you hear the Holy Spirit whisper the words, 'Blessed are those who draw on God's strength, who endure trials and crash through quitting points–for they shall receive the crown of life.'"

When God speaks the pungent language of suffering in our lives, these women have much to teach us. Once Hope wins in their lives I've watched them getting ready for "coronation day." They lift up their heads as they endure the trials and crash through the quitting points waiting for their reward—the crown of life. God is honoring their faith and drawing them to Himself. He is blessing them to rise above, to overcome the age-old prejudices and evils ingrained in the fabric of their cultures. And He is empowering them to raise up their children in God's ways.

Through my tears of joy I can see the rainbow of God's hope crowning them someday with the Crown of Life, but even now fulfilling Isaiah's prophesy, "You will also be a crown of beauty in the hand of the Lord, And a royal diadem in the hand of your God," (Isaiah 62:3). These royal diadems are shining for God in their huts and villages, in concert halls and churches, in radio stations and prison cells. And even though the world sees their predicament as an unending hopelessness, we at Project Hannah see it as an endless hope! Dr. Billy Graham, one of the greatest of God's agents of change summarizes what I have endeavored to convey in this simple book this way, "Let people feel the tears in your heart and the compassion in your soul. Jesus wept over Jerusalem. . . . How often do we weep when we see poverty, abuse and suffering? As believers we have a special responsibility to have compassion on the poor, the sick, the oppressed, the hungry, the outcast, and those torn by terrorism and war all over the world. You don't have to get up and preach . . . You witness by the way you live, by your attitude–your love, care, and compassion toward people, no matter their race, religion, or ethnic background. If we put hands and feet to the gospel message and live it out daily, those around us will see it for what it is–the Truth that transforms." Yes, and they will also see God's awesome miracles when ***hope wins!***

Epilogue

> Open your mouth, judge righteously, and defend the rights of the afflicted and needy.
>
> —Proverbs 31:9

I have a prayer for you . . . that these amazing stories will not just touch your heart but also challenge you to do whatever God is asking you to do. That you will use whatever He has gifted you with for His purposes.

Faith is His precious gift to every believer! The smallest faith, even faith the size of a mustard seed, has the power to move mountains. When you exercise this gift of faith, you pray expecting God's intervention in extraordinary ways. I would ask you to consider becoming a Project Hannah intercessor, joining thousands of others in this amazing worldwide prayer movement for suffering women and the "girl child."

Interceding intelligently and corporately has been one of the greatest joys of my life. I have seen God transforming ordinary intercessors over and over again into "world changers" as they do this powerful work of prayer! To pray, after all, is the most powerful thing we can do. Project Hannah's prayer calendar is translated into more than forty languages. It is posted on the Project Hannah web site: www.projecthannah.org. Those who sign up to receive the monthly prayer calendar join thousands of intercessors praying for the same request each day—a 24/7 wave of prayer around the globe.

You can also change the world by reaching out to the women in your own community. God planned that we be His hands and feet; His mouthpiece spreading hope and His healing love to broken people around us. Open your eyes to see their need and your heart to bless those God sends your way.

Lastly, you can invest financially in what Project Hannah is doing around the world. In this way you can take part in speaking hope and salvation to women everywhere through radio, the Internet, and other narrow-casting media.

I believe this book was placed in your hands because God wants to widen your horizons and take you out of your comfort zone; to experience His heart of compassion and His mighty saving power! If you decide now to give a couple of minutes a day to stand in the gap and pray for women in your community and around the world, then this book has fulfilled its purpose.

Only when we accept Jesus' gentle bidding to do His will and perhaps even go to the ends of the earth to share His hope and love, will we see how hope wins in our own hearts! I pray you'll join Him as I did. Believe me, it will take your breath away!

About the Author

A native of Brazil, Marli Spieker is Founder and Global Ministry Director for Trans World Radio's (TWR) Project Hannah, a ministry of compassion, encouragement, and hope serving the needs of suffering women worldwide.

Marli and her husband, Edmund, began their ministry with TWR more than 40 years ago. From 1969 until 1983, Marli and Edmund pioneered and directed TWR's Brazilian partner organization, before accepting the invitation of TWR founder Dr. Paul Freed to join TWR's international staff in North America. Then in 1997, while serving with TWR in Asia, the Lord called Marli to start Project Hannah after she witnessed oppressive situations faced by women on the streets of Singapore.

Today, Marli has become an advocate and authority on the plight of women worldwide. She has traveled extensively, ministering to women in more than 65 countries. A dedicated wife and mother of three, Marli makes her home in Cary, North Carolina.

A ministry of Trans World Radio (TWR), Project Hannah's passion is to encourage, educate, and empower women to seek God and to instill His lasting hope in their hearts. Project Hannah offers compassion, encouragement, and hope to suffering women worldwide through:

- A global prayer network of thousands of intercessors in more than 100 countries praying through a monthly calendar distributed in more than 40 languages.
- An awareness campaign that encourages passionate prayer by sharing the needs of women.

• *The Women of Hope* radio program airing in more than 50 languages across the globe.

To learn more about Project Hannah, or to receive the newsletter or monthly prayer calendar please go to www.projecthannah.org or call 1-800-456-7897.

Speaking fluently in more than 200 languages and dialects, TWR exists to reach the world for Jesus Christ. Our global media outreach engages millions of people in 160 countries with biblical truth. Since 1952, God has enabled TWR to help lead people from doubt to decision to discipleship.

Together with international partners, local churches, and other ministries, TWR provides relevant programming, discipleship resources and dedicated workers to spread hope to individuals and communities around the globe. Whether using high-powered radio to reach people in the Middle East and Latin America, streaming content to Internet users in Asia and Europe, or visiting face-to-face with listeners in Africa, TWR leaves a lasting spiritual footprint.

1-800-456-7897

www.twr.org

TWR P.O. Box 8700 Cary, NC 27512-8700